Business Mechanics

Can you fix it?
A nuts and bolts guide for
small business owners who
want to go places

by
Jerome Jacobs

CANI Training Limited
Auckland, New Zealand

Published by CANI Training Limited
Auckland, New Zealand

National Library of New Zealand Cataloguing-in-Publication Data
Jacobs, Jerome, 1971-
Business mechanics : can you fix it? : a nuts and bolts guide for small business owners who want to go places / by Jerome Jacobs.
ISBN 978-0-473-21667-2
1. Small business—Management. 2. Success in business.
3. Organizational effectiveness. I. Title.
658.022—dc 23

Version 1.0

Author Online!

For updates and more resources, visit Jerome Jacobs' website at

www.BusinessMechanicsBook.com

This book is for all the entrepreneurs and business owners who are working to the brink of burnout in trying to make a success of their dreams. May this book set you in the right direction...

Contents

INTRODUCTION 1

TAKING STOCK: Are you ready for your journey? 5

FINANCIALS: Do you really know how your business is going? 19

PROCESSES: Does your business have a User's Manual? 31

SALES: Does your prospect want the sports car or family wagon? 41

MARKETING: Which brand of vehicle should you choose? 51

RECRUITMENT: Do you have the right people on your bus? 61

SERVICE CREW: Who are the support crew on your journey? 71

JEROME'S STORY: About the author 79

INTRODUCTION

If you're reading this, then chances are you're already a business owner, or you're thinking about starting your own business.

Well, it's time to fasten your seat belt - you're in for the ride of your life... and you're the one in charge of the controls!

Sometimes the journey will be fun...

Ah, there's nothing quite like the feeling of cruising along the open road with the wind blowing through your hair, and the sun warming your skin.

Everything's humming along quite nicely: the sales are rolling in; your team's working in perfect harmony; the customers are happy... even the accountant is happy!

Buckle up! You're the one in control of your business.

In short: your business is running like a well-oiled machine.

And this is the kind of business that most people dream of: a business that seems to run by itself. So that you, the business owner, can spend more time setting up other commercial enterprises (if you're a serial entrepreneur), or perhaps you'd like to spend more time holidaying on tropical beaches.

But achieving this kind of dream is more challenging than most people realise when they first set out. For many business owners, their business isn't so much a well-oiled machine, as one that splutters and threatens to explode.

Business is rarely a long, flat road...

... it is far more likely to feel like this!

Sometimes the journey will be one of ups and downs...

Sometimes your business will feel quite the opposite of a well-oiled machine. The road might be so bumpy you'll feel as if you're on a rollercoaster. Or maybe your staff are so dysfunctional and your finances in such poor condition you'll wonder if your business will break down somewhere along the way.

Or maybe you thought you knew which direction you're heading in, but the further you go, the further away the destination seems to get.

There are so many things that could affect your journey, it can be hard to know what to fix first when things start going wrong.

That's where this book comes in; it's designed to help you become your own business mechanic.

What you'll get out of this book

This book will take you through many of the different aspects of a business:

▶ **Taking stock:** Are you in the right business? Is your business roadworthy? Do you have the correct training and experience to be successful in your industry? Or are there some skills gaps that need filling?

▶ **Financials:** Just like the speedo in your car tells you how fast you're going, there are certain key numbers that tell you how well your business is performing. Find out what these numbers are, so you can always tell if your business is cruising along or likely to stall.

▶ **Processes:** If you find yourself doing the same things over and over again, then this chapter will be a huge time saver.

Discover how to become your own business mechanic to keep your business humming.

▶ **Sales:** Sales are what fuels a business... but are you getting enough sales? And are you converting enough prospects into customers?

▶ **Marketing:** In order to get sales, you need to do marketing... marketing is like the wheels that keep your business moving. Discover how to give your marketing momentum, so that you can reach your destination faster.

- ▶ **Recruitment:** driving a business by yourself is hard work - chances are you'll need a team to help you. The key to making this work is ensuring you've got the right person in the right seat.

- ▶ **Service crew:** no matter how good our team is, we can't do everything in-house: sometimes we need a helping hand from professionals such as Accountants and Business Advisors. They're often the people that give your business a bit of oomph to propel it along.

You'll be encouraged to look at these aspects from a new perspective that's all about diagnosing what's going wrong, so that you can begin to fix it. It's about putting you back in control of your business, so you can keep truckin' in the direction you want.

How to use this book

First things first: you need to embrace that you're the one driving your business, and that you have control over it.

Taking a 'victim' mentality where you blame the economy, blame your staff, or blame your competitors isn't going to work. You'll need to put all that aside, take a nice, deep breath of air, and roll up your sleeves so we can fix this thing.

I started life as an auto mechanic before I turned to business advice, so you can be assured that I can help you fix your car *and* your business!

Jerome Jacobs

**Jerome Jacobs –
Business Mechanic**

Jerome Jacobs, Business Mechanic
- Auckland, New Zealand

CHAPTER 1

TAKING STOCK: Are you ready for your journey?

~~~~~~

What you will learn in this chapter:

▶   This chapter is designed to make you think:

▶   Are **you** ready for the journey ahead?

▶   Do you have the right business **skills** to get to your destination?

▶   Is your business the right **vehicle** to get you there?

▶   What is your **destination**? Do you have a road map of how to get there?

▶   Do you have an information **dashboard** to tell you how you're progressing?

~~~~~~

Are you ready for your journey?

Before we start buzzing down the road of business opportunities, let's just do a quick check that you have everything you'll need to get you to your destination. This is an overview - we'll cover each item in turn in more detail:

1. **You - the driver:** You're the one taking responsibility for the journey; you're the person in control. Are you ready for the challenge?

2. **Driver's licence:** No, not a real driver's licence, but a metaphorical one. In other words, do you have the right skills, qualification and experience to get to your destination?

3. **Vehicle:** Is your business the right vehicle to get you to your destination? In other words, does your business have the right structure? Or do you need to make some changes to your business set-up in order to make your journey? In other words: is your vehicle road worthy for the journey ahead?

4. **Road map:** You wouldn't embark on a journey to a new destination without a map, would you? Likewise, you need a road map (or plan) to help you steer your business in the right direction.

5. **Dashboard:** In your car, the dashboard has a number of gauges that let you know if all's well or not. You need to have similar at-a-glance information at your fingertips in your business, and that's what the dashboard does.

DO YOU HAVE EVERYTHING YOU NEED FOR YOUR JOURNEY?

1. DRIVER

2. DRIVER'S LICENCE

4 & 5: ROAD MAP & DASHBOARD

3. VEHICLE

Check and make sure that you have everything you need for the journey ahead.

1. You are the driver...

It's important that you realise that where you take your business is totally in your hands. You are the driver, and all the decisions are yours.

So before you set off, let's just do a quick reality check on a few things. There's nothing worse than finding out too late that you're on an expensive journey to somewhere where you don't want to be. Ask yourself:

- Are you ready for the journey ahead? Are you willing to be **responsible** for the actions you take and the decisions you make?

- **Why** did you go into business? It's important to identify what motivated you to start this journey, as chances are this is what will continue to motivate you in the future.

- Is your industry **viable**? In other words, is there sufficient demand for your product or service? There's nothing worse than being on the road to nowhere.

- Do you **enjoy** your industry and your business?

2. Do you have the right driver's license for your vehicle?

... Or to put it another way, do you have the right skills and experience for the business structure you've chosen?

For example, when we're kids we learn to ride a bicycle. When we're a bit older, we learn to drive a car. Some of us are happy to stick with that; other people might go on to obtain a special licence, such as for trucks or aeroplanes.

Similarly, we might start out in business as an owner-operator. But when we take on staff that adds a whole new dimension, because all of a sudden you're responsible for recruitment, performance reviews, processing wages, and so on. In short: you're suddenly required to be a manager and a leader.

Being a manager or leader takes skills: but many business owners change their vehicle without much (if any) up-skilling.

Be honest: do you have the necessary skills to lead your current (or desired) business structure? Or would you benefit from some specific kinds of management training?

After all, it would be mighty hard to fly an aeroplane without any instruction. Similarly, it's just as hard to suddenly be in charge of a team of employees without any instruction. (Yet all too often, people are thrust into that environment without any considerations of the repercussions.)

No one would expect you to fly a plane without the right training… so why should you run your business without the right training?

3. Is your business the right vehicle?

Is your business structured in the appropriate manner to service your industry? And will your current business structure help you to achieve your goals?

Perhaps your business is too large? Or too small? Or located in the wrong place geographically?

It's important to look at your company's position within your industry.

But what about your company itself: what is its mission, and its culture? Does the current mission and culture serve your business - or is it holding it back? Are these values going to be relevant for your future journey - or do you need to revisit them?

It's vital that the way your business is organised has to be suitable for the journey ahead.

Here's an example of a client who realised he wanted to upgrade his proverbial vehicle, and he followed a certain sequence of steps to get to his destination:

Example: an automotive workshop

This client had worked as a hands-on mechanic for many years, and eventually he bought his first automotive workshop, which was strategically located on a busy main road.

Business was humming along nicely, thanks to the workshop's location and the client being well known in the local community.

The client realised that his business was 'okay', but that it had the potential to be even better. What's more, he had dreams of opening more workshops... but he knew that he didn't have the business skills or knowledge to do that right away. He needed to up-skill, and think more like a business owner and leader.

In order for this client to move his business in the direction he wanted to, I worked with him to make a number of changes:

Systems and processes: were streamlined and defined, so that they could be replicated across each new workshop.

Recruitment processes: taking on board new habits with regard to managing staff and hiring a Manager.

Financials: setting up some Key Performance Indicators (KPIs) so that the client could have a clear overview on how each workshop is performing.

How did this work out? At the time of writing this book, the client has purchased a second workshop and has turned it into a profitable business. He is now looking at buying a third workshop.

What can we learn from this? This client has upgraded his proverbial driving licence multiple times: first of all from mechanic to a manager, and then to a business owner of multiple workshops.

The client realised that making these moves would take time: business growth doesn't happen overnight. And he also realised he'd need to learn new skills to enable him to make these transitions.

The client's growing business is thriving thanks to the business owner's diligence and careful planning.

Did you notice how this client grew his business because he'd carefully planned each step? He knew he'd need to upgrade his credentials as a manager and business owner, and 'up his game'. And that's exactly what he did.

Reverting back to the car analogy, this business owner has started the journey of having a single car (or single auto workshop) to having a fleet of cars (number of auto workshops).

Multiplying and growing a business is something that many business owners dream of.

But what if you don't want to upgrade your vehicle?

Not ready to upgrade your vehicle? That's fine! But do take a close look at your current business model. What worked fine for you a few years ago, might not be so fine now. Technology, competitors, industries, customers - they're changing and evolving all the time.

This is important to acknowledge and embrace if you want your business to perform well. Out-dated business practices can cost you more than they're worth. In many cases, upgrading things works out more cost-effective in the long run - provided that your business is worth investing in. (Which goes back to the point at the beginning of this chapter, where you read about making sure that the industry you're operating in is viable.)

Just look at the car industry itself as an example of how things have changed. In the early 1900s cars were started with a hand-cranking mechanism, where the driver had to manually 'wind up' the car with a handle. Nowadays, starting a modern car is as simple as pressing a touch key. There certainly isn't a market for car hand-crank handles any more!

So even if you don't want to upgrade your business at present, be sure to keep your ear to the ground to make sure you're fully in touch with industry trends and consumer demands.

The money that you invest in your business needs to give you a return: if it's not doing that, you need to have a look under the hood to find out why that is. In other words, is your vehicle road worthy?

Is your vehicle road worthy?

Here in New Zealand, cars have to be tested every six months to ensure that they're safe and road worthy. That testing process is called a Warrant of Fitness - you may have something similar but with a different name in your own country.

When you take your car for a Warrant of Fitness, the mechanic has a checklist to see if all the parts of the car are functioning properly. And by making sure that everything's functional and safe, it should mean fewer accidents and mishaps due to neglect.

A Warrant of Fitness for your business is wise, too

Just like your car has a Warrant of Fitness, it's important to check your business regularly too, to make sure it's safe. After all, when a business fails, there are casualties: staff, suppliers, and the families of everyone involved suffers. A failing business may not be life-threatening, but it can still shatter livelihoods, homes and relationships. That's why a business warrant of fitness is sensible if you want to avoid breaking down.

It's prudent to check that your business is fit and healthy.

Have you ever looked at someone else's business and said something like, "they're always going broke", or "they're always losing staff" or "they're always late paying their bills"?

If you've ever found yourself thinking that, there's a good chance that this business has a weakness in one (or more) specific area. By giving your business a check-over with a Warrant of Fitness, you're able to identify the weak points in your own enterprise.

How to carry out a Warrant of Fitness for your business

As your Business Mechanic, it's my job to carry out a Warrant of Fitness for your business. I'd do this:

- At the outset, to check that your vehicle is safe for your journey; and
- Every three months thereafter, to ensure that your vehicle is always in good shape.

The areas this Warrant of Fitness covers are as follows:

- Debt
- Capital items
- Stock or materials
- Overheads
- Insurance
- Marketing
- Sales
- Finance
- Production
- Organisation
- Personal.

~~~~~~

4. Road map

Do you have a specific goal in mind for your business? Or are you happy taking the scenic route, and wondering where you'll end up?

The driven business owner will often have a very specific goal in mind. But the most challenging step involves figuring out the most efficient way of getting from A to B. That's where the road map comes in, as it prevents you from taking wrong turns and dead ends.

Road map elements

In business, the road map generally consists of certain goals. And it's our progress against these goals that lets us know how close (or far) we are from our destination.

These goals will include targets for the following:

- **Financials:** Profitability and other performance data is the primary basis on how we measure the success of a business. But in order to achieve that financial success, there need to be goals for the things that allow us to make money in the first place. The key financials to monitor are: gross profit, debtors, creditors, profit and loss.

- **Sales:** Sales revenues have a huge influence on profitability, so the wise business owner will set sales targets. These include: sales revenue, number of leads, value of leads, number of sales, sales conversion rate.

- **Human Resources:** It's people who are responsible for running the business and making sales, so it is a good idea to measure how well these human resources are performing. The most common measure here is the productivity per staff member.

- **Overheads and debt:** Sales made by a skilled sales force aren't enough for a business to be profitable: the astute business owner will need to keep an eye on the business' expenses. It's this overview of all the different elements of a business that let the business owner know if there's enough gas in the tank to get to the destination.

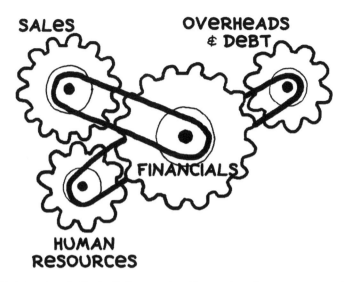

SALES

OVERHEADS & DEBT

FINANCIALS

HUMAN RESOURCES

It's vital to check that all the parts of your business are running in sync and moving you forwards.

Different types of road maps

Have you ever done a road tour in a foreign country? Back in the days before GPS and satellite navigation systems were invented, we had to rely on paper maps. So for a road tour you had to purchase a number of maps: a general map of the country as a whole, and then some street maps of the major cities. Why? The country map doesn't contain enough detail for you to navigate comfortably around the huge cities.

In business, you'll want different road maps too. If you only have a five-year plan, the goals will seem too distant to make much sense - you need things on a more practical scale. Most successful business will have the following plans:

- **Quarterly plan:** task-based plans and goals.

- **One year plan:** short-term goals.

- **Two to five year plans:** this is where things start to get exciting, as these medium to long-term goals may include taking on investors; multiplying the business onto new sites; franchising/licensing; and taking on a General Manager.

- **The Big Hairy Audacious Goal** (often called a 'BHAG' for short): where do your dreams dare take you? It's vital that you verbalise this dream, as it's this vision which will help to motivate your staff and attract talented people to your business.

But just like paper road maps get out of date when new roads are built, or old roads closed, the business road map changes too. It's important to keep on top of your plan and treat it as a 'live' thing that needs nurturing and tending to.

How do you do that? The most important thing is to check that you're making progress towards these goals. And you do that by keeping one eye firmly focused on your dashboard's gauges.

5. Dashboard

In your car, the dashboard has a number of gauges that let you know if all's well, or if the poor car is over-heating or if it needs more gas. These gauges give you instant feedback on what's happening.

You need to have similar at-a-glance information at your fingertips in your business, and that's where the idea of a dashboard comes in. It's vital that you identify the most crucial performance indicators of your business, and that you check these on a daily basis.

Relying on quarterly (or worse still, annual) reports from your Accountant are a guaranteed way to face breakdowns and disasters on your journey. This historical data is of little use: you need to know what's happening *right now*. After all, you wouldn't want the fuel gauge in your car to have a three-month time lag!

Which gauges should you be looking at?

You should be looking at *all* the performance measures you've identified on your road map.

And every quarter you should take an in-depth look at what's happening. Just like a car's engine is made up of a number of moving parts, so is your business. Sometimes you need to delve deep under the hood of your business to find out which cog isn't turning, or which piston isn't firing.

Here are some of the leading questions I ask at review time - and business owners often have an interesting answer to some of these. So have a good look at this list, and see if there's anything here that's sounding alarm bells or giving you food for thought:

- **Profit centres:** How is each profit centre performing? What are the margins of each of them? How are each of the profit centres impacting on each other?

- **Billing:** What's the ratio of billable hours versus total hours worked? How does time reporting take place? Is billable time rounded up - and if so, how much? Are there any minimum charges? How promptly are invoices issued? How accurate are the invoices? Are there any other revenue streams that haven't yet been explored, such as on-selling other products or services?

- **Pricing:** Who's looking at costing and pricing structures? Is any discounting activity taking place? Are there any costs that could be reduced?

- **Financials:** What is break-even point? What are the profit levels? How is the business's performance tracking against budget?

- **Debt:** Is debt restructuring required? Is debt being managed adequately?

- **Inventory:** How is inventory being managed? How much cash is tied up in stock? Could terms of trade with suppliers be improved?

- **Personal:** How many hours is the owner working?

Be sure to pay attention to anything that's sounding alarm bells; it will be having a knock-on effect on the other cogs in your business. And keep checking those gauges, constantly.

~~~~~~~~~~~~~~~~~~~~~~~~~~~~~~~~

Quick tip ...

▶ The average person in New Zealand has a life
expectancy of just over 80 years... that's 4,160 weeks.
Are you making the most of each and every week, and
are you getting closer to your destination?

~~~~~~~~~~~~~~~~~~~~~~~~~~~~~~~~

Key points from this chapter

▶ **You** are the driver, responsible for the direction your
business takes.

▶ To get to your destination, you need the right **business
skills**.

▶ Your business must be the right **vehicle** to get you to
your destination.

▶ You need a road map to get you to your **destination**.

▶ You'll also need an information **dashboard** to tell you
how you're progressing.

~~~~~~~~~~~~~~~~~~~~~~~~~~~~~~~~

CHAPTER 2

FINANCIALS: Do you really know how your business is going?

What you will learn in this chapter:

▶   What your rev counter says about your **Margins**.

▶   What your speedo says about your **Productivity**.

▶   What your fuel gauge says about your **Cash flow**.

How to understand your engine gauges *before* the warning lights come on

Aren't cars wonderful things? Not only do they get you to your destination, but they're designed to do so as effectively as possible. To help you complete your journey safely, they even have gauges and warning lights to help you avoid any problems. If you're low on fuel, or if there's some kind of mechanical fault, your car will tell you.

It's just as important for your business to have warning gauges

After all, just like your car gives you an early warning of any problems, you should have a warning of poor performance in your business too. There are three specific gauges that you should use as early-warning systems in your business:

▶   **1. Rev counter:** relates to your margins

▶   **2. Speedometer:** looks at your company's productivity

▶   **3. Fuel gauge:** monitors the cash flow.

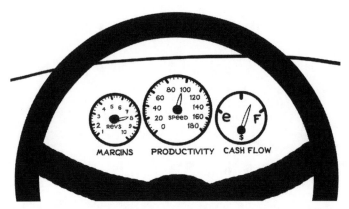

Keep your eyes on the dashboard to make sure your vehicle reaches your destination!

We'll look at each of these three gauges in turn.

1. Rev counter: Margins

When I start working with business owners, one of the first things they usually ask me is, "Can you help me get more sales?" ... Or in other words, "Can you help me get more profit?".

This is the right question to ask me! But in order to answer the question, the business owner first of all needs to understand what 'profit' actually means.

What is profit?

Profit is derived from sales, less the cost of achieving those sales:

Sales – Cost of Sales = Gross profit (Money) and Gross Margin (Percentage of that same money)

('Gross profit' means the profit you make before you pay tax. That's the way we usually measure profit.)

Here's an example of a gross profit calculation:

If you make $100 in sales, but the cost of sales is $40, then your gross profit is $60. Or putting it mathematically:

$100 - $40 = $60

From that we can work out your margin:

To earn $60 in profits, you had to make $100 worth of sales. That means that your margin (also known as 'gross margin', because it's based on your gross profit) is 60%. Or to put it mathematically:

$60/100 \times 100 = 60\%$

Knowing your margin percentage is very important. You should work it out for your own business.

Let's look at an example of why it's so important to consider the gross profit and gross margin.

Example: an electrical contracting business

An electrical contracting business asked for a review of how their company was performing. The company consisted of 13 electricians, two admin people and two managers, as well as the owner.

Part of their business Warrant of Fitness involved analysing the company's monthly profits, and to see if they had healthy profit margins.

To do that, I needed an understanding of the different clients the company serviced. This consisted of trade, commercial, industrial and retail clients. The company had some pricing systems in place, but there was no true measurement of what the actual cost of a job was. Both the labour and materials costs weren't accurately tracked, so the business owner had no idea how well the business was performing for each client type.

So the business owner had some homework to do: to set up the systems to measure the individual gross profits on each client type.

We also looked at how the charge-out prices of the materials were being calculated, and we realised that this was done on a mark-up basis rather than a margin basis. (The two are vastly different... we'll look at that later.)

Because the materials were being charged on a mark-up basis, the company was significantly under-charging for them. What's more, the materials were only being marked-up at 25% (significantly below the industry average of 65%), and labour was being charged out at below the industry average too. Plus there was no charge for travel time, admin time or management time.

Let's look at some numbers...

Here's a job that the electrical business charged the client $250 for. That included:

- 1 hour of labour @ $60 per hour

- $100 of materials with a 25% mark-up (i.e. they were sold for $125)

Mark-up = (Sales price − Cost price) / Cost price x 100

Let's now work out the gross margin:

Gross Margin = (Sale price − Cost price) / Sale price x 100

($250 - $185) / 250 x 100 = 26% Gross Margin

The conclusion? The business was seriously under-charging and even though the company was very busy, it was nowhere near as profitable as it should be. That's reflected in the very low level of gross margin.

This example illustrates why back-costing is important to see how much margin is required to ensure that all of your expenses are covered.

When I start working with a new client, very early on we look at making very small changes to increase the company's profits. Just making a periodic 1% increase to labour rates and material margins can make a very dramatic impact to a company's profitability... without them even having to achieve more sales.

At the same time, be sure to review your terms with your suppliers. If you can get even small discounts from bulk buying; that too can have a very significant impact on your profitability.

Summary of rev counter elements:

- Sales value

- Cost of sales (cost of materials, etc.)

- Mark-up or margin charged on materials and labour

- Gross margin percentage.

2. Speedometer: Productivity

This is all about comparing actual hours worked versus billable hours. Time reporting is an important element in most businesses, and accurate record keeping and invoicing is vital if you want to maximise your profit levels.

PRODUCTIVITY

Once you've paid all of the week's wages you should take a look at:

- How much time has been charged out

- Sick leave

- Public holidays

- Annual leave

- Warranty work/call-backs and other re-work hours

- Non-chargeable work (e.g. admin time)... this last one is usually the real profitability killer!

Here's a fictitious-but-realistic example as to how you could analyse the actual hours worked versus the chargeable hours over a month:

	Total hours	Chargeable hours		'Lost' hours that can't be charged for			
	Time sheet hours paid	Charge out hours	Quoted job cost hours	Re-work hours	Sick days	Warranty hours	Uncharged hours on time sheet
Adrian	136	111.5	7	4	4.5	3	6
Craig	112.5	95.5	8	0	0	0	9
Dave	109	81	3	4	0	0	21
Jared	117.5	79	22.5	10.5	1	1.5	3
Jono	101.5	89	0	5	0	0.5	7
Kalim	155.5	136.5	0	9	0	0	10
Total	732	592.5	40.5	32.5	5.5	5	56
	(100%)	(80.94%)	(5.53%)	(4.44%)	(0.75%)	(0.68%)	(7.65%)

Chargeable hours = 86.47% of total hours worked	Unchargeable hours = 13.53% of total hours worked

If this company's charge-out rate were $75 per hour, re-work alone would have cost this company $2,437.50 for the month.

The total value of these unchargeable hours for this month would be $7,425. It's vital that these unchargeable hours are monitored and controlled, as they can significantly erode the profitability of a business.

Let's look at why this kind of measurement was so vital to the electrical contracting business we met earlier in this chapter:

Example: an electrical contracting business

Once we got a handle on the margins, we were able to put a system in place to review the weekly activity. This involved implementing measuring practices with proper planning. When this was underway, we were able to measure the work productivity of the business.

The electrical contracting company was losing between $10,000 and $12,000 a month on average due to uncharged hours.

This measuring process highlighted hours that were being paid but not being charged or allocated to tasks. Once this problem had been identified, the business owner was able to discuss it with the production team. Together, the business owner and his team were able to tackle the problem of charging for hours that had previously been lost.

The discrepancy between hours worked and hours invoiced is a major issue for most businesses. But until you start looking at the numbers, you won't know just how much it's impacting your profitability.

Hint: look at the numbers! Chances are that addressing these issues will make a very significant impact to your company's bottom line profits.

Summary of speedometer elements:

- Hours worked
- Billable hours
- Invoiced hours.

3. Fuel gauge: Cash flow

If the goal of a business is to make profit, then cash needs to be flowing in at a greater rate than it's flowing out. Hence the importance of measuring cash flow, as cash is the fuel to help you reach your destination. That's why you need a proverbial 'fuel gauge' to keep tabs on all the different price and money elements of a business.

CASH FLOW

These financial elements to keep track of include:

- Costing and pricing structures
- Discounting versus increasing prices
- Break-even point
- Actual performance versus projected performance
- Costs
- Are customers paying you on time?

Someone in the business needs to be monitoring these factors continually.

Where's the money?

Have you ever had the situation where you come to the end of the month; print out your Profit and Loss statement and go, "Yippee I made a profit!". But then you look at your bank account... and it's empty.

So where did the money go? There are a few areas where the money can be hiding, especially if you're in the kind of business that either gets delayed payments or holds stock.

Imagine that you have 30-day payment terms with your supplier; but your customers have 60-day terms. That means that your cash gap can easily span 90 days... that's nearly three whole months!

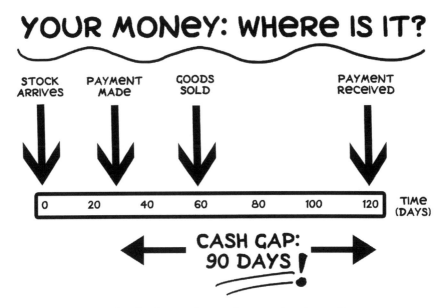

YOUR MONEY: WHERE IS IT?

STOCK ARRIVES

PAYMENT MADE

GOODS SOLD

PAYMENT RECEIVED

| 0 | 20 | 40 | 60 | 80 | 100 | 120 | TIME (DAYS) |

CASH GAP: 90 DAYS!

What's the cash gap in your business?

Here's how to fix the cash gap

- Review stock levels: are you holding too much stock?
- Are you invoicing promptly enough?
- Are your customers paying you quickly enough?
- Are you paying your suppliers too quickly?
- Are you drawing too much money from the business?
- Do you have business loans that are affecting your cash flow?

Notice that these factors are all process related. So if you're having cash flow issues, always ask yourself, "what is the process or system that relates to that part of the business?". Then look for a system correction before a people correction.

Let's see how the electrical contracting business dealt with their cash flow discrepancies to see how that works in practice:

Example: an electrical contracting business

When dealing with large, commercial clients, the cash flow was working very favourably for the electrical business. That's because they had good systems in place, i.e. robust Terms of Trade which were properly followed and implemented.

However, the retail side of the business didn't enjoy quite such a good cash flow. The retail business was made up of smaller residential clients, who (a) weren't invoiced very promptly, and (b) these clients took their own sweet time to pay. What's more, the admin cost in following up these late payments was very high.

How these late payments were addressed

The late payments were addressed with some team training for on-the job invoicing and debt collection.

The company made a small investment in a mobile electronic payment system, whereby clients could pay on-the-spot with their credit card or debit card.

The company also revised their incoming telephone scripts to let prospects know up front what the payment terms were. This meant that they were far less likely to argue the payment terms later on.

What was most important of all in making this work was to measure the team's performance, to ensure they were following the system. After all, not only does the system need to help a business achieve its goals, but systems are implemented by people. So the people need to be monitored too, if the system is to be successful.

Summary of fuel gauge elements:

- Speed of invoicing
- Speed of supplier payments
- Stock levels.

Key points from this chapter

▶ What your rev counter says about your **Margins**.

▶ What your speedo says about your **Productivity**.

▶ What your fuel gauge says about your **Cash flow**.

CHAPTER 3

PROCESSES: Does your business have a User's Manual?

What you will learn in this chapter:

▶　　**What** kinds of things you can (and should) systematise.

▶　　**How** to go about systematising your business.

▶　　The importance of **evolving** your systems as your business changes and grows.

Systematise the routine tasks

A vehicle needs its engine and chassis to be kept in good working order if it's going to reach its destination safely. That's why new cars are sold with a User's Manual; this tells the owner how to perform key maintenance tasks.

Unfortunately businesses don't come with a ready-made User's Manual: you need to write your own! This might seem onerous, but if you're serious about keeping the wheels turning (profitably), it's a must.

Imagine if every time you had to service your car you had to figure it out from scratch. That would be pretty time-consuming, right? It makes sense to document such a routine task.

The same thing applies in your business: taking a little bit of time up front to document routine tasks is a huge time-saver in the long run. It makes the routine task so much easier to implement by your team.

Effective systems can save you and your team both time and money. By 'system' we're not talking about computer systems or programmes. No, this kind of 'system' is about the various tasks required in running a business – but doing those tasks in an organised, planned and coordinated manner.

Carrying out tasks in a planned way means that things are done consistently, regardless of the team member who's carrying out the tasks. This makes it easy for new team members to get up to speed quickly in their role.

Systems exist to help with routine tasks. Of course, not all tasks in a business are routine. So anything that can't be systematised (because it's not a routine task) will need a greater degree of human involvement. But by identifying what can be systematised, you'll be using your human resources far more efficiently. The alternative to systematisation? That would involve employing more people, i.e. taking on more overheads and reducing your profit.

~~~~~~~~~~~~~~~~~~~~

Remember...

▶   Systems run your business: as the business owner, you have invested in the system.

▶   People run your systems: it's up to you to choose the people who implement these systems.

▶   You lead your people: it's your vehicle... so drive it well!

~~~~~~~~~~~~~~~~~~~~

What kinds of tasks can be systematised?

The following pages will give you an idea of what kinds of tasks can be systematised. Of course, not all processes will be relevant to all business types – and there could be something really crucial that isn't listed here. It's up to you to brainstorm what's important, these are just ideas to help you get started.

Office and admin systems

- Answering the telephone: does everyone answer the phone in the same way?

- How do you deal with receiving and opening the mail?

- Purchasing and maintaining office supplies and equipment.

- Faxing and emailing: are stationery templates being used? Are there policies on email use?

- Dealing with incoming and outgoing goods.

- Backing up and archiving data, and checking that the back up data is complete and functional.

New product development systems

- Developing new products and seeking legal protection from them. Developing and protecting intellectual property.

- Developing packaging and collateral material, such as catalogues and sales aids.

- Developing manufacturing methods and processes.

Systems for manufacturing and inventory control

- Selecting vendors, including a tendering process.

- Determining product or service warranties offered.

- Establish product or service pricing and margin levels, with retail and wholesale pricing.

- Establishing an inventory re-order process and establishing minimum and maximum inventory levels.

- Reconciling physical inventory with accounting records, i.e. stocktaking processes and procedures.

Processing and tracking orders

- Taking orders by mail, fax, phone or online.

- Logging the order and customer details in a computer system.

- Fulfilling and packaging the orders.

- Confirming the order and shipping details before delivery.

- Sending the orders, including a management system for freight, couriers and vehicles.

- Order tracking systems for shipments.

Invoicing and accounting

- Invoicing customers for the orders.

- Receiving payments for the orders and crediting customers for payment (whether cash, cheque or credit card).

- Monitoring credit control and age of accounts.

- Starting the collection process for outstanding receivables.

- Purchasing procedures and approvals required for Purchase Orders.

- Payment process for supplies and inventory.

- Petty cash procedures.

- Managing the accounting process with daily, weekly, monthly, quarterly and annual reports. Including cash flow statements, balance sheets and profit and loss accounts.

- Processes to ensure that monthly and yearly budgets are logged and that targets are met.

- Reviewing borrowing needs: are they secured and available?

- Tax procedures and payments to Inland Revenue. Includes reporting payroll taxes, sales tax, superannuation and withholding payments.

- Complete a weekly bank reconciliation and having a daily banking system.

- Maintaining an asset register including depreciation values.

Customer service

- Returns procedures: for inventory and customer orders.

- Logging and responding to customer complaints.

- Replacing defective products or performing other warranty service obligations.

- Measure quality and professionalism of service delivery.

- Customer feedback systems and measures.

Sales and marketing

- Negotiating, drafting and executing client contracts.

- Creating a strategic marketing plan and processes for identifying key marketing strategies to follow.

- Ensuring that a consistent brand message is communicated, with corporate usage guidelines for branding.

- Designing and producing promotional materials, printed and online.

- Developing sales leads and prospects.

- Creating an advertising plan, including setting goals, KPIs and budgets.

- Creating a public relations plan, including setting goals, KPIs and budgets.

- Creating a direct mail plan, including setting goals, KPIs and budgets.

- Developing and maintaining a customer database, and systems for communicating with your existing clients.

- Developing and maintaining a website.

- Analysing and tracking sales statistics:

  - Continuously measure number and origin of all leads

  - Measure conversion rate for each salesperson

  - Measure your average dollar sale for every team member

  - Keep a record of your profit margins.

Human resources

- Recruitment procedures, including job descriptions, position descriptions and recruitment methods and scripts.
- Training employees: initial induction programme and on-going training and development.
- Payroll process and frequency of payments.
- Systems for planning and managing leave, e.g. annual leave, sick leave, compassionate leave, etc.
- Career planning, performance reviews and pay reviews.
- Company vision and mission statement and culture.
- Company and individual team member goals and performance indicators.
- Conflict resolution and disciplinary procedures.
- Contingency staffing plans.
- Redundancy systems.
- Health and safety procedures and requirements, including emergency and evacuation procedures.

General operational systems

- Managing insurance needs and ensuring adequate coverage levels.
- Managing and storing records (paper records and computer data).
- Maintenance of equipment, including premises, plant, office, warehousing, computers, etc.
- Maintaining investor and shareholder relations.
- Information flow processes: internal and external.
- Ensuring legal security.
- Developing a business plan for planning and managing growth.
- Maintaining and designing telephone and electrical systems.

- Maintaining and upgrading office equipment.

- Planning permits and fees.

- Ensuring physical security of premises and people.

Seven steps to systematisation...

1. **Identify all your processes.** What are you doing on a regular basis that a lower-paid team member could be doing if it were systematised? Or is there anything in your business you hate doing, and would love to hand over to someone else? This could involve any task, be it admin, sales, marketing, financial or operational in nature. Use the lists earlier in this chapter to identify *all* the different processes in your business.

2. **Prioritise the processes to systematise.** In most cases, it won't be feasible to systematise every process in the business at once. In that case, it makes sense to review the list of processes you've written and identify the priority tasks to systematise.

3. **Flowchart your processes.** This involves identifying each major step of the processes you've identified, and in which order these tasks happen. By putting this into a flowchart diagram, you'll see how it all fits together in a very visual way. Don't worry about going into too much detail at this stage, just write down the key steps.

A company manual makes it easy for anyone to join your business and get to work right away.

4. **Document how it gets done.** This is the detailed stage. Get the team member who is currently doing the job to write down every step in performing the task.

5. **Test the documented steps**. The person who's written the steps in performing a task should then get a colleague to follow their instructions to see if they can do the job. If this colleague has to ask any questions, the team member who wrote the tasks initially should add these steps to the document. The idea is that a person totally new to the job can follow the written instructions without needing extra help or assistance.

6. **Measure using key performance indicators (KPIs).** Typically, these KPIs will be the top five measures that show system performance. These KPIs will relate directly to the KPIs of the person doing that role. For example, if it's a sales process, KPIs might include number of leads; number of sales; average sales value; sales conversion rate, and so on.

7. **Allow the system to change and grow.** Any systems documentation needs to be a 'living' document, i.e. it should grow and evolve with the business. After all, things like computer programmes are always changing, so it follows that any system or process might need to change too. It's up to you to ensure that your staff always keep the process up-to-date. Essentially, it is your responsibility to make sure that the systems are (a) being implemented, and (b) are relevant to the business.

Some final tips on systematisation...

▶ Place someone in charge of the systematisation project. Start to flow chart the simple areas first.

▶ Don't over complicate systems or people won't follow them.

▶ Use lots of photos, videos, screen shots etc. with the description. This may be as simple as taking a computer screen capture or videoing someone doing the task. This will make the systems much easier to follow.

▶ Document your system in a policies and procedures or operations manual in an easy to access format. And make sure everyone knows where it is and references it regularly!

▶ Remember that your processes will need to evolve with your business: if not, the process won't get used by your staff, and they'll start improvising, and you'll be back to Square One. Make sure that regular system upgrades are planned and documented in your corporate calendar.

You will be amazed at the improvements in your business when you start to implement systems and procedures.

What's more, if you intend to sell your business in the future, you'll be adding a lot of value by having all your processes systematised and documented as it will make life so much easier for the new business owner.

Key points from this chapter

▶   What kinds of things you can (and should) systematise.

▶   How to go about systematising your business.

▶   The importance of evolving your systems as your business changes and grows.

CHAPTER 4

SALES: Does your prospect want the sports car or family wagon?

What you will learn in this chapter:

▶　A good sales person is a **solutions provider**.

▶　How to create a **sales process** that'll provide consistency and clarity throughout your business.

▶　Why you need to address your sales **conversion rate** in order to improve your company's profitability.

Why a good sales person is a solutions provider

Fact: no business can survive without sales.

Yet so many business owners visibly shudder at the mere mention of the word 'sales'. So many business owners have mental pictures of pushy, sleazy sales people. The kind of sales person that will say just about anything to clinch a deal.

But how many sales people are actually like that? Think back to a time when you were a customer, and had a positive buying experience with a sales person. Chances are that the sales person was helpful, knowledgeable, and took an interest in your needs and concerns. And once they'd listened to you, they were able to recommend the product or service that best suited your needs, right?

In fact, this helpful sales person is at the other end of the spectrum to the pushy, sleazy mental image. Correct?

So why create that unattractive mental picture of a sales person? It's time to get that out of your head, and replace it with the mental picture of a helpful, knowledgeable sales person. That positive mental image will serve you far better in your business.

A good sales person:

- Is **knowledgeable** about their industry as a whole, as well as the products or services they sell. For example, a car salesman will know about his competitors' vehicles as well as those manufactured by his company.

- Will **listen** to customers to identify their needs, concerns, and budget. For example, a car salesman will quickly establish whether the client is looking for a family car, commercial vehicle or sports car – and the budget for it.

- **Acknowledges** the customer's objections and responds positively to them. For example, if a client had concerns about the safety aspects of a car, the salesman would show them the vehicle's safety features and maybe even provide comparison charts to similar vehicles.

- Is **customer-focused** and has a strong sense of customer service. For example, the car salesman will take his time serving the customer and allow them to take the vehicle for a test drive. They have his undivided attention whilst in the car showroom.

- Leaves the customer feeling **happy** and educated. For example, the car salesman's customers drive away happy in their new vehicle.

This approach to sales is known as consultative selling. In my view, it's the best (and only) way to sell. It is dignified, and – most importantly – it works!

It's a win-win situation, as both the sales person and the customer is left with a good feeling after such a sales experience.

Remember: sales should be enjoyable – for all parties.

Consultative selling is a pleasant experience for both the client and the sales person.

Sales are also essential for your business

Half the time and energy of every great business should be invested in sales and marketing. This will give you a steady flow of quality leads, that are to be professionally and systematically followed-up.

The goal? To achieve conversion into a life-long business relationship with your customer.

People are the basis of every business

It's important to consider the lifetime value just one customer can provide. Here's an example of this in action:

Example: the lifetime value of a customer

It's wise to think about customers in terms of a life-long relationship, rather than just how much they're spending with you each month or each year.

I worked with a client with a horse-training business for two years. This client then introduced me to a business owner with a building franchise: he also became a client, and we worked together for two years. And then this client introduced me to other clients.

In short, the horse-training client contributed $50,000 to my business (through direct and indirect means) over a number of years.

How was this achieved?

Achieving this was simple: it's nothing more than treating people with respect; and doing a good job for them. Sometimes it's worth asking clients for referrals too: they may well have a friend or colleague in need of your product or service.

Remember, people like to do business with other people, so if you work at building good business relationships it can pay you back many times, and for many years. This is the most cost-effective kind of lead generation you can get. Plus the lead is pre-qualified, as they've already been told that you do a great job!

How to make lead generation less costly

Let's face it, lead generation (i.e. marketing) is a costly exercise. And leads are just one aspect of the sales equation:

Leads x Conversion Rate = Sales

However, many companies who review their sales levels work at just increasing the number of leads. This is often the wrong way to go: you can get far more impressive results by improving the Conversion Rate. (And usually that is quite inexpensive compared to the cost of generating leads.)

Example: a kitchen unit manufacturer

As well as manufacturing kitchen units, this company also had a showroom on their premises. Their business was growing rapidly, and they were spending vast amounts of money on their marketing. But they weren't measuring any aspects of their sales or marketing, so they had no idea which activities were working for them, and which were a waste of money.

What's more, because the company was growing so rapidly, their approach to sales was a little sporadic. Customers weren't receiving a consistent buying experience, and follow-up calls to prospects were rarely implemented because things were just too disorganised and chaotic.

Together we created a flowchart for their entire sales process. (You'll see an example of a sales process flowchart on the following pages.)

The various stages of the sales process correlated with the company's database so that each stage of the process could be measured and analysed.

Key stages of the sales process also included checklists. For example, the most important checklist was related to ensuring that each prospect was given all the relevant information to make their buying decision.

Another important stage in the sales process was the follow-up call from a salesperson.

The result? Profitability went up by 15%, simply as a result of having (and implementing) a measurable sales process. And that's without the company having to spend an extra cent on marketing, they were simply getting better results from their existing investment.

What kinds of things improve sales conversion rates?

The kinds of things that will improve sales conversion rates vary from business to business. Here are some of the most popular tools:

- Client testimonials: these can be written, or videos, or both.

- Good quality marketing collateral (printed and online).

- Frequently Asked Questions (FAQs) or a similar document, which addresses any objections a prospect may have up front.

- Staff who are trained in sales and customer service skills.

- Ensuring that all sales staff have a sales kit containing sales aids, portfolios, etc.

- Making follow-up calls to prospects.

Is your sales process flowcharted?

It's well worth your time putting your sales process into a flowchart diagram. Why? It helps to make the sales process fool proof! Everyone in your team will be able to see what the steps are, and which sequence they need to be performed in. It's far more visual than words alone.

In order to create your own sales process flowchart, you need to:

1. Identify all the different steps in your existing sales process.

2. Identify the steps that you could include, but aren't currently implementing.

3. Putting all of the above steps into a logical order.

Hint: using sticky Post-It notes can be a good way of working through this exercise.

Once you've got everything mapped out with your sticky notes; photograph them and then type up the flowchart on your computer.

Example of a sales process flowchart

Here's an example of what a sales process flowchart might look like for the kitchen unit manufacturer:

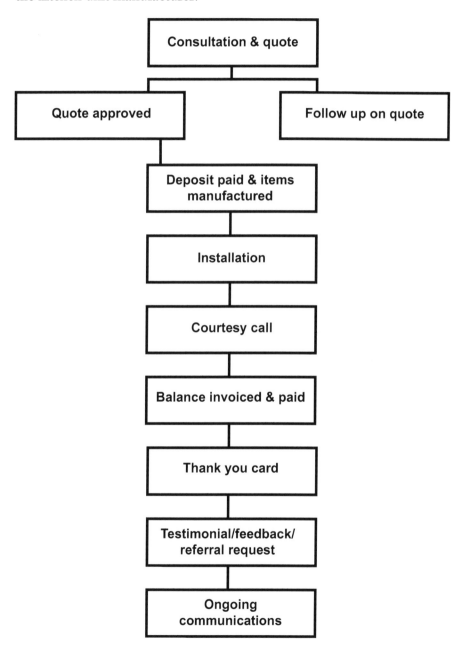

Of course, the sales process flowchart will vary from business to business, so this is a starting point for you to work from.

The flowchart stages that are often forgotten about...

Notice how in the example flowchart there are a number of steps which happen after the transaction is complete? These are activities such as:

- **Making a courtesy call to ensure the client is happy.** This is so rarely done, yet it's a must. If the client is already happy with your product or service, they'll be super impressed at this point. Or if they're not quite so happy, it gives you the opportunity to put things right for them until they are happy.

- **Asking for a testimonial.** Happy clients are usually willing to help with testimonials, as they are happy to help a customer-focused company promote itself. These testimonials are vital for your sales and marketing, and the ideal time to ask a client is when they've expressed happiness with their purchase.

- **Thank you card.** Oh, how rare it is to get something in the mail that isn't a demand for money! A nice greetings card with a hand-written thank you message really gets noticed. It's classy, and it's also a very inexpensive way of making (yet another) positive impression on your customer.

- **Feedback questionnaire.** Take this opportunity to seek feedback from your customer, so you can learn from their buying experience to improve your business even further.

- **Ask for a referral.** How about asking your client for a referral? Perhaps they have a friend or colleague who's in the market for your product or service too?

- **On-going communications.** Remember, it is eight times more expensive to find a new customer than it is to retain an existing customer. Therefore it's vital that you add the client to your marketing database so that you can build a relationship with them, rather than treat the sale as a one-off transaction. Even for the kitchen unit manufacturer, there's the opportunity to sell maintenance and service products once a new kitchen has been installed. In nearly every industry, there's the opportunity to make ongoing sales - and the key to doing that is to stay in touch with your customer regularly.

Many of these 'forgotten' sales process flowchart stages will need to interface with the marketing department. It's vital that sales and marketing work in tandem to achieve the common goal of growing sales... and to achieve a lifelong business relationship with your customer.

~~~~~~

Key points from this chapter

► A good sales person is a **solutions provider**.

► How to create a **sales process** that'll provide consistency and clarity throughout your business.

► Why you need to address your sales **conversion rate** in order to improve your company's profitability.

~~~~~~

CHAPTER 5

MARKETING: Which brand of vehicle should you choose?

What you will learn in this chapter:

► Why it's important to have an appropriate **brand**.

► The importance of being totally clear on your **target market**.

► **Testing and measuring** is the key to profitable marketing.

Brand of vehicle

A brand creates a distinctive way for your customers and prospects to identify you in the marketplace. Look at how important this is in the car industry: there are very strong perceptions related to brands such as Mercedes, Porsche, General Motors, Ford, Toyota, Honda, and so on. We perceive each of these different brands quite differently.

The same applies in all industries: your company's brand sends a clear message to your audience about your position within that industry. And it's up to you to make the most of that, to ensure that your brand is perceived positively by your target market.

Consumers are heavily influenced by brands – so it's absolutely vital that you get your brand message right.

Here are some questions you should ask yourself about your company's brand:

- How clear, distinctive and unique is your brand?

- Does your company have a professionally-designed logo and usage guidelines? Are these adhered to?

- How well-known is your brand amongst your target market?

- Is your brand relevant to just your local market – or does it have international representation?

- Does your brand or logo have any legal protection?

- Is your brand connected with quality?

- Do you have a website? (This is vital in today's market, no matter the size of your business or your industry.)

- Do you have a computerised database? (This is vital in communicating with your customers and prospects.)

Non-frustrating marketing

Have you ever seen a driver who's tired of steering the wheel of their business? Or perhaps the vehicle is just spinning its wheels and not going anywhere.

Often these sorts of issues stem from the axle connecting sales and marketing being out of alignment.

The tired driver might be driving after the wrong customers. Either the company's marketing offer is wrong for the target market. Or the target market isn't responding to the company's brand. Or something else is out of alignment.

Or when the wheels are spinning without the company getting anywhere, the marketing could be falling on deaf ears. There might be a lot of marketing activity, but it's just not getting seen or noticed by the target market... and that's expensive. Lots of expense plus minimal sales does not make a good business model.

These sorts of marketing frustrations are all too common, and a big reason for company owners feeling burnt-out and frustrated.

How can they fix this problem? They can fix these marketing woes by having a clear understanding of what drives the company's profit, such as:

- Identifying your ideal client and target market.
- Having appropriate branding that your target market will respond to positively.
- Knowing how to reach your target market in a cost-effective manner.
- Creating and testing offers that your target market will respond to.
- Testing and measuring the different marketing channels and offers, so you can see what's working – and what isn't working.

Testing and measuring marketing

There are numerous ways in which you can test and measure your marketing. But the single most vital question you should be asking everyone who contacts your business is:

"How did you hear about us?"

Be sure to ask this every time, and log the results in such a way that you can go back and analyse them easily. That'll soon teach you which marketing channels are working.

If you wanted to take that a step further (and you should!) then you could then compare that to:

- Number of sales per marketing channel.

- Value of sales per marketing channel.

- Conversion rate per channel.

Acting on that data will most definitely stop the "wheels spinning without going anywhere" sensation, and help your marketing move up a gear.

We'll look at a real life example of a client who was able to move their marketing (and sales, and profitability) up a gear or two by taking this kind of analysis-centred approach:

Example: a landscaping company

This landscaping company is a small business, with a team of 11 people. They operate at the premium end of their industry, targeting high-earning residential clients in upmarket suburbs.

The primary objective of this landscaping company was to grow their business by finding more customers. Together we identified that a two-pronged approach would be needed:

1. Lead generation: finding more prospects.

2. Maximise conversion rates: converting prospects into customers.

Finding more prospects

When you need more prospects, those prospects shouldn't just be any Joe Bloggs: you should be looking for your ideal client (target market).

By analysing previous sales activity, the landscaping company identified that their ideal client lived in either a beach house or in the outer city fringes. They were homeowners with high incomes.

Developing marketing collateral

Rather than targeting these prospects with the usual sales brochures or flyers, it was decided that a more value-added approach would suit this type of client. Something that provided some tips and advice, while at the same time promoting the landscaping company's skills.

The result: a multi-page newspaper-style brochure was created.

The benefit of this style of marketing collateral is that it can be used in a number of different ways, such as trade shows and networking events. The newspaper-style brochure gave the landscaping company real credibility, and provided them with enough space to outline the benefits of their landscaping services.

Implementing the newspaper-style brochure

The landscaping company used their newspaper-style brochure for various campaigns over a year. The cost for 14,000 copies was as follows:

Design costs:	$1,975
Printing:	$2,273
Distribution into local newspaper:	$1,753
Internal labour:	$462
Total cost:	**$6,463**

So how did the brochure perform?

Over the course of a year, the brochure generated 133 leads and 14 sales, with a value of $247,496.

Plus those clients generated a number of referrals with a value of $28,699. That brought the total sales value from the brochure to $276,195. That means that the brochure costs had been covered 42 times over!

This example shows that the landscaping company was very smart in designing marketing-collateral to suit their goals. Many business owners make the mistake of developing a brochure, and then trying to find a purpose for it. You'd be far better advised to think of the marketing activity first, and only then consider which kind of marketing collateral will best do the job. You also need to consider the kind of collateral or media your target market will respond to.

What to include in your marketing collateral?

Once you've figured out what kind of format your marketing collateral should take, you need to make sure that the piece covers the four key questions that a potential customer may have:

1. **What's your company?** Answer: include a company profile.

2. **Who are you?** Answer: include a personal profile of each sales person or key team members.

3. **Can I trust you?** Answer: include testimonials from satisfied customers.

4. **How can you help me?** Answer: outline your product or service, and how it benefits your customer.

Brochures tell; people sell

There's more to marketing than producing pretty printed brochures and websites. They simply tell readers what's on offer. In order to generate sales, most businesses need to implement a number of person-to-person interactions to make sales. This could include:

- Sales team visits, pitches and proposals
- Cold calling
- Affiliates and strategic alliance partners doing your selling for you
- Networking groups
- Trade shows.

These person-to-person selling activities all take careful planning and implementation to get the best possible results. And once again, it's vital to measure the costs and results to see what's working – and what isn't working.

Let's take another look at the landscaping company to see what's worked for them.

Example: a landscaping company

We'll look at two different activities the landscaping company undertook with regards to person-to-person selling:

1. Strategic relationship development
2. Trade show stand.

1. Strategic relationship development

Based on their previous marketing activities, the landscaping company realised that strategic relationships were a low cost and highly profitable way to grow their sales.

The team had a brainstorming session to identify which companies had the ideal end-user client, and also had strong business ethics and values in place.

Example of a successful strategic relationship

The landscaping company completed a project for a large building company. As a result, they formed a great relationship with the Project Manager and also the Quantity Surveyor

The landscaping company then implemented marketing campaigns in order to maintain their relationship with them. (After all, 'out of sight is out of mind'... so it's worth spending time and trouble to make sure you stay at front of mind of the people who matter.)

The landscaping company took the Project Manager and Quantity Surveyor on a fishing trip; gave them mulch for their gardens; gifted them a Christmas hamper; and offered them a finder's fee for work they passed on.

Did this marketing investment in strategic alliances pay off?

Most definitely!

Over the space of just one year, the Project Manager provided $605,000 in work and referrals. And the Quantity Surveyor $174,000 over the same time period. This is quite a significant amount of work for a small business with 11 employees.

The finder's fee and related marketing activities cost the landscaping company just over $3,100 over that time period. That investment has paid them back 251 times: this is very smart marketing indeed, with its low cost and high return.

2. Trade show stand

If you ever hear it said that exhibiting at a trade show isn't profitable, there's a good chance that the person telling you that hasn't approached this marketing tactic properly.

To get good results from a trade show stand, there's a lot of background work involved, mostly centred around identifying what kind of person attends the trade show, and ascertaining if that person is in your target market.

The landscaping company identified an annual event that they wanted to have a stand at. The whole team visited this show one year, so they could observe the attendees; to see what kind of companies were exhibiting; and to speak to these companies to see what kind of results they were getting.

Having confirmed that this particular trade show would be a good one for them to exhibit at, the landscaping company carefully planned their stand. They got their team and their suppliers behind them, and put a lot of thought into the offer they'd make on the day.

How much did the trade show stand cost?

The landscaping company spent $4,183 on their trade show stand. This covered:

- Stand fees
- Materials (water pump and pavers)
- Flyers
- Prize
- Labour

They were then able to sell the water pump at their stand at the end of the show for $1,000, so that brought the cost down to $3,183.

But did they make any sales?

Absolutely! 177 people entered the prize draw, so each person was treated as a sales lead and followed up. Four of these people converted into customers.

While that might not be a very good sales conversion rate, these four sales had a combined value of $50,908. This is a pretty good result for a weekend's work: this marketing campaign paid for itself nearly 16 times over.

Just to put these results into context...

The landscaping company in the example has a very high average dollar sale. So they require very few sales in order to make a good profit margin. If your company's average dollar sales value isn't so high, then these kinds of activities are unlikely to yield the same kind of results for you. It's all about finding the formula that works for your business.

What's more, this landscaping company is a very marketing-savvy company that's been testing and measuring their marketing performance for a number of years. They did not achieve these results overnight; rather, they were able to work towards getting this kind of marketing performance over a period of time.

It goes to show that if you put the time and effort into measuring, analysing and planning, there are some very profitable marketing campaigns your business could benefit from.

Key points from this chapter

▶ Why it's important to have an appropriate **brand**.

▶ The importance of being totally clear on your **target market**.

▶ **Testing and measuring** is the key to profitable marketing.

CHAPTER 6

RECRUITMENT: Do you have the right people on your bus?

What you will learn in this chapter:

▶ Why it's important to consider the different **personality types**.

▶ Overview of a recruitment **process** that works.

▶ The financial **cost** of recruiting the wrong person.

The importance of having the right people in the right seats

Recruitment is something that many business owners just don't enjoy; yet one of the most common ways of growing a business is to enlarge by taking on staff. More people equals the potential to earn more income.

So how do you know how to hire the best people or the right people for your business? I see the frustration in business owners' eyes all the time and get the glazed look often when it comes to choosing new team members.

All that most business owners see is the cost of having the wrong people on the their bus. Or they're in shock from what they might have heard from other business owners who have gone through the process. Or they've had their own bad experiences with recruitment.

This may be true for you... or maybe you're just impatient, and will recruit the first person that comes along, rather than recruiting the *right* person.

Since most folks go for the first cab off the rank, it's often a waste of time because they did a poor job at the beginning of the recruitment process.

The key part of the recruitment process involves looking at the different personality types and how these come into effect with the tasks and responsibilities of the job. That means that first of all you have to understand yourself: your personality, and what motivates you. Only then should you look at the position you're recruiting for, and decide what kind of personality is best suited to that role.

Recruitment isn't about randomly putting 'bums on seats'... it's about making sure you've got the right bum on the right seat, and that's why personality profiling is an important part of the process.

DISC personality profiling

One of the best personality profiling systems I've come across is DISC. The reason why I rate DISC so highly is because it's easy to understand and easy to implement. In fact, once you're familiar with it, you don't even need other people to complete a form to be able to understand their personality type: it is possible to make reasonably accurate off-the-cuff guesses!

The DISC personality profiling system is based on two dimensions:

- Introvert vs. Extrovert

- Task focused vs. People focused.

Here's what the four DISC personalities look like:

Extrovert

D Driver:	**I** Influencer:
• Determined • Demanding • Ambitious • Risk-taker • Competitive	• Enthusiastic • Confident • Outgoing • Popular • Optimistic
Natural leaders who love to be in control. **At work they like to:** • Have the freedom to make decisions • Have challenging assignments	Excellent communicators who interact well with others. **At work they like to:** • Focus on building relationships with others • Have freedom to express their ideas
C Compliance:	**S** Steadiness:
• Conscientious • Cautious • Controlled • Systematic • Perfectionist	• Reliable • Patient • Loyal • Peacemaker • Softly-spoken
Precise, organised people who tend to follow the rules. **At work they like to:** • Work on tasks requiring precise detail and accuracy • Critically analyse the situation	Compassionate people who are sincere and like to help others. **At work they like to:** • Consider how issues affect the team • Have a routine and work at a relaxed pace

Task Orientated (left side label) • *People Orientated* (right side label)

Introvert

Be clear and focused at interview time

Before you decide to fill the seat on your bus (or in your business), we should be very clear about the individual and why it is that they want to join your organisation. It is vital that you take this opportunity to ask the tough questions up front. This pays huge dividends; especially if you consider how much it could cost you if you were to employ the wrong person. The quality of questions will always help you with the quality of answers, meaning a better quality decision.

Take a walk together at the interview...

One of the best recruitment tips I've heard is to take a walk with a future team member. While you're walking, keep check on the pace that they are moving at: are they walking faster or more slowly than you?

If the candidate is walking faster than you, you're probably dealing with a fast-paced person in general. This person is a fast thinker; a fast mover; motivated; ambitious; focused and driven. There's a good chance that this person could push and challenge you if you were to employ them. This person would make a good manager.

On the other hand, if the candidate is walking more slowly than you, you're probably dealing with someone who likes to do tasks at a steady pace. They pay attention to details, and they may not like change. This person could be a good team member, provided that they're not so slow they hold the team back.

What if they're walking at the same speed as you? That's a good sign that you're in sync with each other... which may or may not be ideal, depending on the level you're recruiting at.

Get to know the candidate as well as you can

If you can, try and spend time in the candidate's environment before engaging them. This is particularly relevant if it's a senior role you're recruiting for, such as a manager or business partner.

You'd be amazed at what someone's partner, spouse or even family members will tell you about the prospect of them becoming a key team member.

Do some of these techniques seem a bit whacky to you?

Some of the recruitment ideas in this chapter might be very new to you.

You should know this: if you don't change the system or process of hiring that you've been using thus far, then you'll simply get more of what you've already got.

In other words, if you want your recruitment process to have better results, then you need to alter your existing process.

What makes for a good recruitment process?

I've sat in on hundreds of interview sessions. In these sessions, I've often wondered why the business owner hasn't asked more powerful questions, and what the consequences are of asking week or vague questions. It doesn't then surprise me when those candidates are recruited, and three months later they're considered 'problem' employees. It's not the employees' fault at all; it's down to a lack of care in the recruitment process.

Here's a proven recruiting and induction system based on the following principles:

1. **Attract a large pool of applicants:** that way you're more likely to find and attract the right person.

2. **Implement multiple levels of screening:** you'll waste less time in lengthy interviews with under-qualified candidates.

3. **Skills testing:** Once you've short-listed the candidates, observe them carrying out the key tasks of their potential job in real time. That way you're far less likely to be surprised on their first day.

4. **Personality profiling:** Use a personality profiling system (such as DISC) to ensure you hire the right kind of person for the job.

You may consider doing group interviews, as this is very effective if you are looking at filling a less skilled position. (You wouldn't want to do this for a General Manager role, for example.)

Also get your key team members involved in the interviewing process, and ensure that they ask the short-listed candidates some probing questions.

Overview of the recruitment process

Take the pain out of recruiting with this recruitment process overview!

The time and energy you put into the recruitment process will dictate what you get out of it, so it is well worth following all the steps.

Important: this checklist is written with New Zealand employment laws in mind. Be sure to observe the laws and protocol in your own country!

1. Generate leads for the position

"Leads"? Isn't that a sales term?

Yes... and it's relevant to recruitment too. After all, you need to advertise in order to get attention, and then make sure that the best leads convert. In other words, you have competitors out there, namely other firms that are also recruiting. It's therefore vital that you promote your company and your role in a way that's enticing as possible. (The approach of "they're lucky to have a job" doesn't work if you want to recruit the best candidates.)

- Develop a job description and advertisement to include the roles and responsibilities, skills required, and whether the role is part time or full time. Also mention any perks, such as a company car, health insurance, staff discounts, uniform provision, clothing allowance, pension plan, and so on.

- Identify lead sources, both internal and external. Use all your network contacts (work and personal) and consider offering a finder's fee. You may also wish to consider engaging a recruitment agency or head hunter.

2. Shortlisting candidates

- Develop a shortlist of candidates, and check the references of your shortlisted applicants.

3. On-site screening of leads (test drive)

- Arrange group or individual on-site screening, which should include skills testing. Once your shortlist is down to two to four candidates, involve your key team members in the de-selection process.

4. Final interview and offer to hire

- Draw up the interview shortlist, and make sure you ask each candidate the same set of questions. Then rate the candidates, and rank them in order of preference. Next it's time to carry out some personality profiling, such as DISC.

- Negotiate the salary and make an offer of employment. Make sure both parties sign the employment agreement.

5. Induction

- Provide the new employee with a thorough orientation programme to the company.

- Identify the new team member's professional development process.

6. Performance Review

- After the new employee's induction, review their performance every two weeks for the first two months.

- After the first two months, performance reviews should then be completed every three months, with seven KPIs to review each time.

If you follow these steps, you'll be well on the way to taking some of the pain out of the recruitment process.

The cost of recruitment...

It's no exaggeration to say that recruitment can make or break your business. It's an area that you need to pay a lot of attention to, or you run the risk of paying a huge price for hiring the wrong person.

Let's take a look at what it might cost to lose and then replace one employee. (The numbers are indicative.)

Step 1: Recruitment and employment costs

  = $7,500 (Recruitment agency fees or advertising, interviewing time, relocation expenses, etc. Some research shows that it takes the equivalent of 6 weeks of a manager's time)

Step 2: The cost of employing a temporary worker while you fill the position

= $6,000

Sub-total: this is the physical cost of loss and replacement

= $13,500

Step 3: The cost of unproductive time

= $7,500 (training the temp and training the new person)

Step 4: Miscellaneous expenses

= $1,750 (admin, secretarial, compliance etc.)

Step 5: The cost of the impact on customers

= $2,500 (lost orders, dissatisfied customers, time delays, broken relationships)

Add up the costs in steps 1 to 5:

Grand Total: this is the true cost of loss and replacement

= $24,650

But wait, there's more...

What if after two months the person still hasn't "got it"? You now have to follow the termination process then start all over again. Your costs have just doubled, not to mention the on-going disruption to your business and other staff while you look for another person.

The financial impact of replacing employees

The cost of replacing employees does not show up in the monthly reports, but it has a drastic effect on the bottom-line of your business through lost productivity, effectiveness and efficiency. That's especially true if you make the wrong hiring decision for the position.

Although it might take some time and trouble to follow the recruitment process outlined in this chapter, it could save you a massive amount of time, money and stress if you do.

Key points from this chapter

▶ Why it's important to consider the different **personality** types.

▶ Overview of a recruitment **process** that works.

▶ The financial **cost** of recruiting the wrong person.

CHAPTER 7

SERVICE CREW: Who are the support crew on your journey?

What you will learn in this chapter:

▶ The kinds of people you want on your side as they'll help you **succeed**.

▶ The kinds of people that will **hold you back** on your journey.

▶ The importance of taking an **objective view** of your support networks.

"You will be the same person in five years as you are today except for the people you meet and the books you read."

Those are the words of Author and Motivator Charlie 'Tremendous' Jones, who was a strong believer in learning from the people around you. That's why it's important to actively consider the network you have around you.

What do we mean by 'actively considering' the people around you? It means:

- Identifying whom you can learn from.

- Identifying any gaps in your network – and actively finding people to fill those gaps.

- Knowing whom to ignore.

Your wealth network

These are the people who will help you be successful:

(a) Resource network

These are advisors you can call on... and this wouldn't normally include your mother! Rather, your resource network should consist of people who have more knowledge than you in a specific area – and who are happy to share this knowledge. These will be your go-to people for when you need good advice.

(b) Opportunists

In this context, opportunists are people who see opportunities and love talking about them. They're a great source of ideas and information.

(c) Financiers

The biggest resource these people have to offer is their money. If you offer them the right opportunity, they will be sure to invest.

You may well find that one person is in more than one of these categories, and that's fine. For example, your Opportunist may also be your Financier. Conversely, you may need multiple people to fit the 'resource network' category, such as a good accountant, lawyer, and so on.

The important thing is that you do know people who fit these categories: they're going to be vital on your business journey.

It's also important that you cast a critical eye at the quality of your advisors. For example, is your accountant really giving you good advice? I've come across many clients where the accountant has given them poor advice (such as to "work harder") when the client really needed to work smarter by tweaking systems, reviewing pricing, and so on.

Your accountant is probably one of the most important relationships you can have in your business, so make sure that they're providing you with a clear strategy and tactics to help you achieve solid growth. If they're not doing that, it's time to move on to find someone who *will* do that for you.

Every business owner needs good service crew to support them in their journey.

Support networks

(a) Peers

This is all about rubbing shoulders with the kinds of people you'd like to have as your peers. They're people who set a positive example for you, and people you'd enjoy spending time with. These should be people who've achieved success in their own business. There is a lot that can be learnt from spending time with such positive role models that have taken a journey similar to the one you're embarking on – and have reached a successful destination.

(b) Supporters

This is where your family and friends fit into the picture. They don't have to give you advice or money: all they need to do is say the kind of things that'll make you feel good about yourself and your journey.

Production network

(a) Managers

These are the people who you feel have the right attributes to run a business or project of yours… And it may not even be a business you have today!

(b) Team

While the 'team' person isn't someone you'd want running your business, this is someone you've identified who would be a good employee. They may have specific skills or talents that you'd like to use.

Example: my friend the General Manager

I have a good friend with a great skill in turning struggling companies into successful, profitable organisations. What's more, this friend is continually up-skilling himself, and he's a very talented individual.

So when I come across business owners requiring a good General Manager, this friend has gotten the job a number of times over the years.

Think: do you know anyone like this, who'd make a great manager? Keep them at front-of-mind, you never know what kinds of opportunities will present themselves in the future.

Poverty network

(a) Distracters

These people are often extremely well meaning… but they'll do anything to distract you. For example, they may always be asking you to go out drinking with them, spend lots of time with them, or ask you to work for them. In other words: they've got their own agenda, and it's not compatible with yours.

Now there's nothing wrong with having distracters, after all, they could be your family or closest friends, but just be aware that they are distracting you, and keep that in check as much as you can.

(b) Doomsayers

As soon as you come up with an idea these people will throw cold water on it. They've always got some reason why you shouldn't do what you want to do.

The solution: identify that they are doomsayers (rather than advisors or supporters) and ignore them!

(c) Doubters

This category can be harder to spot. Whilst they won't necessarily have a good argument against your idea, they may ask questions that are actually cloaked in destructive criticism. For example, they may ask, "Are you really sure you should do that? Are you really sure that makes sense? What happens if you did that and it failed?"

Rather than providing constructive criticism, their comments are negative, and this eats away at your confidence.

(d) Passengers

Unlike the negativity of Doubters or Doomsayers, Passengers are quite happy for you to do what you want to do. However, these people will just tag along for the ride without contributing their share of the petrol money, so to speak. They'll gladly share in your glory, but won't add value or contribute to your success.

Have the faith and confidence in yourself to let these people go; chances are they will try to make you feel guilty when you do, but just remember the journey you are on, and have belief in yourself.

How does your support crew stack up?

Now that you know the different types of networks and support crew types, have a think about the people around you.

Not enough people in your Wealth, Support and Production networks?

In that case, it's time you networked more – and in different circles. Are there any business groups or associations you could visit or join? Or a local Chamber of Commerce, or similar group? It's time to spread your wings, my friend!

Too many people in your Poverty network?

These sorts of people (even if unintentionally) keep your wealth away. The way that they think is a negative influence on you getting to your destination. How you deal with that is up to you.

~~~~~~~~~~~~~~~~~~~~~~~~~~~~~~~~~~~~

Key points from this chapter

▶ The kinds of people you want on your side as they'll help you **succeed**.

▶ The kinds of people that will **hold you back** on your journey.

▶ The importance of taking an **objective view** of your support networks.

~~~~~~~~~~~~~~~~~~~~~~~~~~~~~~~~~~~~

CHAPTER 7

JEROME'S STORY: About the author

Everyone has a history, but history does not need to limit your future

When I was a child, I had no idea of the journey ahead of me… a journey that's been fun, frustrating, exhilarating, terrifying. In short: pretty much your basic entrepreneurial journey!

Looking back, I learnt lots of good lessons from my parents. I grew up in Capetown, South Africa, and although my parents weren't wealthy, they worked hard. There was always food on the table, clothes on our back, and a yearly camping holiday.

Dad did whatever work he could to earn money; he was a motor mechanic (and a very good one at that) and a real jack-of-all trades. He earned extra money from buying and selling vehicles and having a fishing business: he did whatever it took to support his family.

Learning about relationship building

I learnt a lot from dad about the art of relationship building. From a young age, I rode in the car with him to deliver freshly-caught fish to his clients as gifts. Even though I was just a boy, I realised that this act was somehow tied to the fact that he was never short of clients at his auto workshop.

Though he knew how to work hard and make money, dad never focused on the systems of a business and was never schooled in marketing or sales. He did these things instinctually, and knew how to operate a decent business.

Through his hard work, my dad became a man of influence in the community; he was a man that others listened to. His business grew thanks to his ability to create long term relationships with others.

I knew I'd need an extra edge to get ahead

Dad's business management techniques served him well, but I had an inkling that I'd need to work differently in order to survive and get ahead. After all, this was the time of computers and capitalism and all sorts of other wondrous things happening in the world. I realised that these big-world events would impact on my own world.

I learned the auto mechanic's trade but it was a hard grind with limited returns.

After a short while I realised that some of my competitors and colleagues were doing things differently to me, such as buying multiple passenger movers. They were making their money and assets work for them. These people enjoyed a different lifestyle to me, a better quality of lifestyle, and I wanted it for myself.

Curiosity and observation paid off

I was full of curiosity as to what my peers were doing differently to make them more successful. So I started to watch them carefully to see what these business owners did that was different to me. This fuelled a lifelong drive in me to become more successful.

At the age of 16, by pure observation, I had learned how to take a little bit of my hard earned money and turn it into more money. I did things like getting other people to do extra jobs, and bought, built and sold cars on the side. That, combined with the work ethic I'd inherited from my dad, served me well. At the time I was working from 9am to 5pm Monday through to Saturday, and never took a sick day. Then, by the age of 21, I had a team working with me, and my workshop was very profitable.

In fact, by the time I was 22 I had more money than I needed and decided to buy my first home. Three years later I upgraded to a four-bedroom house: by today's New Zealand standards that house would be worth close to $1 million.

Three years later I was debt-free, with a thriving business... and I was completely unaware that the golden era was about to end.

Then things started to turn bad...

Without warning, the transportation and mechanical industries began to suffer financially.

Not only was my business about to take a downturn, but life in South Africa was taking a massive downturn in the late 1990s.

The country had become a hotbed of violence and political unrest. One day, completely out of the blue, my uncle was kidnapped from his home. He was in the garage at the time, and my aunt and cousins were upstairs. They were completely unaware of what was going on just metres away from them.

Thankfully my uncle escaped with his life, but I was extremely aware of the need to escape my beloved homeland and go to a place where I could have more control over my life and the destiny of my future family.

In 1999 I married Linda and three short months later we migrated to New Zealand. We set up a new life on Auckland's North Shore and I worked for a year as a mechanic. The lifestyle was easy and laid-back; a complete contrast to how South Africa had become.

The entrepreneurial spirit returns

Like many migrants, the change of scene and new beginnings inspired and motivated me, and I allowed my entrepreneurial tendencies to kick in again.

I formed a partnership in a mobile mechanic business. Six months into the venture we took on a business coach and suddenly, and for the first time in my life, I had someone asking me hard questions and challenging me.

The business coaching process meant that I took a good, hard look at myself. Not just at my business, but also at my life and general direction. This brought about an enormous period of personal growth: it turned my world upside down and made me into a serious student of life.

Business coaching changed everything

The business grew rapidly under the guidance of this business coach, and became successful.

But more importantly, it re-ignited my fascination with business and management. It was very much on a parallel with the curiosity that had driven me to be successful in South Africa, but this time I was learning about systems, structures and processes to create success, rather than me just observing random actions.

I was utterly enthralled by these systems and processes, and I decided that another change in direction was called for. So I relinquished my shares in the mechanical business to my business partner, and re-trained as a business coach.

Change isn't always easy

Re-training sounds so blasé, so casual, but it can take an emotional toll too.

I remember when I was Auckland Airport's international terminal, about to fly to Brisbane, Australia, for my retraining programme. The boarding pass required me to fill in my Occupation. I was literally in a cold sweat with my heart thumping as I wrote 'Business Coach' into that innocuous little box. It was at that point that I'd decided there was no going back: I had to make a success of this, and I vowed never to use my mechanical skills as a fall-back option... even though the career change had required my wife and I to take a second mortgage on our house. This career move was not without its risks.

Up until this particular moment at the airport I had never realised how blessed I was to have married a woman who would not let me live beneath my potential. Just before I'd left for Brisbane, she had told me that I'd better be sure I was doing the right thing, and with the financial risk we were taking, she wouldn't tolerate my failure.

The stakes were high: especially as we'd recently welcomed our first son, Joshua into our family.

I thank God for Linda: I am a better man because of my wife. And I'm a success thanks to her belief in me. Even though she's a tiny lady of few words, Linda continues to give me great insight and definition. Her support in my career change made it a given, that it must be a success.

So how did the business coaching venture work out initially?

The business coaching wasn't just about being successful so my family could be proud of me, but right from the start I was there to get results for my clients.

Nearly half of my clients were couples who were in business together. Very few had business partners or outside investors. In short: they had as much invested in the business coaching as I did.

I have a huge amount of respect for my clients, but that sometimes meant that some tough love was in order for them to achieve their goals. I wasn't there to be a friend; I was there for them to get the profitability and growth results they were after.

Award-winning results

Some of my clients chose to enter Awards… and many ended up winning! I'd never planned on having clients win Awards; I just wanted them to do their best in their businesses.

From 2004 onwards clients were categorised in, and won, "Business of the Year", "Most Innovative Business", "Best Financial Results", "Best Team", "Best Marketing", "Best Emerging Business", and overall "Business of the Year".

Jerome Jacobs (left) with his client, Kelvin Armstrong Auto Repairs, who won a prestigious "Best Small Business Award" in 2010.

I'm very proud of my clients achieving this; they deserve to win. In my view, if you put the most effort in, then you deserve to win at life, and at business.

What about my own, personal performance?

After three years of doing okay, I decided I could still be performing better. The old self-improvement drive was still going strong! So once again I stepped up, and was duly recognised as one of the top one hundred business coaches in the world. I stayed in that position for five years.

During this time, I spent in excess of $150,000 on my education and learning. That's how driven I was to improve myself, and to achieve the best possible results for my clients.

Up until this point the business coaching had been via a large, international coaching company. This served me well for a while, but eventually I realised that I could achieve more than that. Over time, it came blatantly clear that I wasn't so much providing business coaching, as saving the lives of my clients, their spouses, and their kids. This might sound rather dramatic, but have you ever seen first-hand the consequences of a failed business?

A failed business might not look outwardly as bad as a road-crash, where there's mangled metal and physical injuries. But a business failure has other consequences: losing homes, losing confidence, losing hope, going hungry, and having to deal with huge amounts of stress. I help my Church with community work: I've met and helped people in these desperate situations first hand.

But here's the thing: avoiding business failure is totally avoidable in most instances. Often it is a lack of knowledge (or poor implementation of that knowledge) that causes a business to fail.

That's when the simplicity of it all struck me

In essence, running a business is quite simple: it boils down to four key areas: finance, marketing, sales and operations. Whenever I looked under the hood of a business in trouble (or a business that's not achieving its full potential), it always came back to these four factors.

For years I was using car analogies when working with my clients: it's hard to shake off my auto mechanic's roots completely! These analogies meant that business concepts that might otherwise seem abstract, can be explained in a way that's easily understood… even by people who aren't 'car people'.

So I hope that you can use these car analogies successfully in your business. Please, use the tools so that you're your own fully-equipped business mechanic, and get your business firmly on the road to success. You deserve it!

May your business journey be smooth and enjoyable!

Acknowledgements

To my wife, Linda, who is God's gift to me. How grateful I am that your belief and constant strength makes it completely possible to be purposeful to my work and the community. Thank you for demanding the quality of life that you and our family deserve.

To Cornelia Luethi for your patience and understanding in working together on this book. Your standards for detail and being clear that readers do get the value really is appreciated. Thanks also for the cartoons which add character to this book.

To Tina Bogaard for assisting with the research and development: your support is amazing. Nothing is ever too hard for you, and what you suggest is always spot on. Thank you.

To my Team at Rise Advisory for the constant feedback and support. (And yes, Matt Jull, I know that this book needs to look good and not to make any compromises on that!) Thanks for the constant critiques.

And a special thank you to all the clients I've had the privilege of working with over the years - you know who you are! Your stories have added value to this book, and I wish you all the very best in your ongoing business journeys.

Author Online!

For updates and more resources, visit Jerome Jacobs' website at

www.BusinessMechanicsBook.com

Printed in Great Britain
by Amazon.co.uk, Ltd.,
Marston Gate.